PANDEMIC ANIMALS

Anthology of Multilingual Poems

By

Mark Angelo Rivera Damo

Copyright © 2021 Pandemic Animals by Mark Angelo Rivera Damo

ISBN:
Hardbound- 978-621-8261-32-7
Softbound- 978-621-8261-31-0
Mobile/Kindle- 978-621-8261-33-4

Cover Illustrator: Roberto Jose Domion Jr.
Cover Designer: Melvin Pumaras

Published by Poetry Planet Book Publishing House
Arranged by Tess Ritumalta

Please submit all reviews and comments or report errors to markangelo.damo@deped.gov.ph

DEDICATION

We are nothing without our sources of inspiration. They are the winds beneath our wings. Thus, I dedicate this book to:

My mentors Dr. Aida Agustin-Cuanang, Mr. Frank Rivera, Mrs. Ritchelle Blanco-Dejolde, Mrs. Eliza C. Vedania, Mrs. Joean R. Baladad, Mrs. Clarybel Dela Cruz, Dr. Jahnese D. Asuncion, and Atty. Mark Dave M. Camarao;

My friends Jayson D. Adena, Dr. Sherwin P. Palaspas, Mr. Rainier Alvarez, Ma'am Etheldrada Asuncion, Mr. Mark James B. Simon, Mr. Jake Tapallas, Ms. Joharra Acio and Mrs. Lolita B. Valdez.

My brothers and sisters Arnel, Angeline, Mary Joy, and Paul.

My nieces Eneri Amber and Althea Jane.

My special someone (You know who you are. Thanks for motivating me to write.)

My aunts, uncles, and cousins from the Damo and Rivera clans.

My father Angelito in heaven, and my very loving mother Mary Jane who never gave up on me.

The Lord Almighty for being the source of my writing prowess.

The Author

FOREWORD

POETRY. Comes from powerful forces in our universe. A literary genre with the most erratic language that only a sane human can understand but can go insane if not...

POEM. The metaphoric and the endophoric in Iloco and others represent the ethics and prejudices as it necessitates its creativity in the play of words as the Ilocano race fondly hide feelings through linguistic deviations and detours when speaking and writing both consciously and unconsciously.

POET. Mark Angelo Rivera Damo in his first attempt of an anthology of multilingual poems and essays about animal themes and community affairs and experiences talking condescendingly but not explicitly of his limited potentials are proof of wit and awareness of his cosmopolitan environs and world.

Angelo's poetry and his craft show an unusual degree of curiosity, talent, and perspective. New to practically tame and wild animals around him, metaphorized and allusioned to human characters.

Great work of literature.

Growing writer of this generation.

Pride of San Nicolas.

Blood of the Ilocanos.

AIDA AGUSTIN-CUANANG, Ph. D

Language and Literature

UP-College of Arts and Letters 1996

FOREWORD

Of all the uncertainties in this time of the global pandemic, one thing is for sure— this crisis brought out the best and the worst in humanity. We have seen the myriad faces of people in the midst of adversity of such magnitude. We championed kindness and generosity in times of want; we chose to love and understand in times of fear and discrimination; till now we keep trusting and believing in times of confusion and uncertainty. But that is not all, for we also saw ourselves discontent, frustrated, betrayed, and left (or felt) alone.

Our collective experiences during this pandemic are captured in this anthology of poems, PANDEMIC ANIMALS. Written by an accomplished educator, this book is inspired by the cacophony of sounds and sights in the jungle that is the world right now, with each animal mirroring and highlighting the character of humanity who are caught in the middle of a catastrophe, and who, with tooth and nails, are in dire pursuit of survival. The apt and precise use of metaphors, amazingly accented with rhymes in three languages, truly makes this book a must-read for everyone. The use of powerful images and clever wordplay amplifies uneven textures of our lives and exhibits moving, spectral pigments of reflection. This book is an adventure itself, full of vivid words and playful caricatures; comic semblances yet straightforward and powerful indignation. Decades and centuries from now, this masterpiece will surely serve as a literary rendezvous of poets and patrons of literature; a testament of looking back and probing into our fears and frustrations, our sense of family and friendship, and most of all, our sense of self — who are we during these trying and extraordinary times?

Personally, with a modest amount of pride, I congratulate the author, Mark Angelo R. Damo, who is a close friend and who served as Literary Editor when I was Editor-in-Chief of The CTE (formerly Normalite) Bulletin during our college days, for this laudable work of compiling his brainchildren into an anthology. Beyond reasonable doubt, this book is a product of his burning passion for poetry combined with his indomitable spirit and astuteness. Indeed, he lives up to a friend's challenge: "Don't just read, be read."

ATTY. MARK DAVE M. CAMARAO
Educator, Writer, and Solicitor

PREFACE

"You are braver than what you believe and stronger than you seem, and smarter than you think."

This quote from the film Christopher Robin had inspired me to write PANDEMIC ANIMALS, an anthology of multilingual poems, to lift up the Filipino spirit during these trying times of the Covid19 pandemic.

Indeed, this catastrophic virus reminded us of the value of family, the importance of contentment, and the significance of our desirable Filipino values.

With the use of creative metaphors in three languages namely- English, Filipino, and Ilocano, I look forward to inspiring readers to be the best versions of themselves. I would like to remind them that the pandemic cannot stop them from achieving their dreams.

This anthology of poems is a humble accomplishment and a manifestation that we can still do good things despite the pandemic.

I thank the Poetry Planet Publishing House through Ms. Marites Ritumalta, for believing in my art and craft as a writer and for being God's instrument to spread positivity during these challenging times.

This book will forever be a memorabilia of our sweet, sour, tangy, spicy, and salty experiences during the pandemic.

Enjoy reading and be inspired!

TABLE OF CONTENTS

CHAPTER 1-YOU AND THE PANDEMIC POEMS

CHAPTER 2-SALAMIN, BUHAY AT TULA*(MIRROR, LIFE, AND POEMS)*

Chapter 1

You and the Pandemic Poems

PEACOCK

Proud as a peacock
is that envious man.
He thinks he's the best,
The finest among the rest.

Proud as a peacock
is our rich neighbor.
She thinks she has it all,
Didn't think that she might fall.

Proud as a peacock
is your masked friend.
Smiling at you sweetly,
but cursing you so deeply.

Proud as a peacock
is a man of evil intentions.
Covered up by vibrant hues,
but he is full of pretensions!

TURTLE

The pandemic
has a lot of turtles-
things that are slow,
things that don't grow!

First is the internet,
that is so sluggish,
online classes and forums,
now we cannot finish!

Second is vaccination,
that is staggered in motion,
we're like waiting for nothing,
while losing everything!

The last turtle is you,
dormant and static on one side.
Patience is a virtue, yes it's true,
But this time, action will save you!
Waiting for Snow

Her cry is a pain in my ears,
I can't stop my falling tears.
A year ago, my Snow turned cold,
a sad story started to unfold.

Her sweetness is a thing I miss,
To see her again is what I wish.
Her bark still echoes in my heart,
filling that deep and bleeding part.

Reminiscing you my fur baby
is a priceless thing to me.
I'm longing for that warm embrace,
so I'll regain the smile on my face.

WAITING FOR SNOW

Her cry is a pain in my ears,
I can't stop my falling tears.
A year ago, my Snow turned cold,
a sad story started to unfold.

Her sweetness is a thing I miss,
To see her again is what I wish.
Her bark still echoes in my heart,
filling that deep and bleeding part.

Reminiscing you my fur baby
is a priceless thing to me.
I'm longing for that warm embrace,
so I'll regain the smile on my face.

TURTLE

The pandemic
has a lot of turtles-
things that are slow,
things that don't grow!

First is the internet,
that is so sluggish,
online classes and forums,
now we cannot finish!

Second is vaccination,
that is staggered in motion,
we're like waiting for nothing,
while losing everything!

The last turtle is you,
dormant and static on one side.
Patience is a virtue, yes it's true,
But this time, action will save you!

LOVE A CAT WITH ALL YOUR HEART

Love a cat with all your heart
for it will love you in return.
Its loyalty remains to you-
endless and very true.

The pandemic has confined you
in the four corners of your room.
The silence is deafening and blue,
but its meow removed the gloom.

No one is as loyal as a cat,
It will never leave you no matter what,
Though small and useless in other's eyes,
No one surpasses the goodness in its heart.

BUTTERFLY

Not your typical butterfly,
Its wings are broken and cannot fly.
Crawling on the ground hopeless,
Feeding on dirty and rotten flesh.

Indeed not that vibrant one,
Its colors faded and are now gone.
Her happiness is now misery,
no more laughters, no more glee.

LEECH

Crawling like a leech,
this blood-sucking bitch,
even worse than a witch,
doing black and evil magic,
for success to be within his reach!

No, no, ugly amateur leech,
Victory's not as what you think,
Soon, your little dirty tactics
be fought with a stronger antidote,
leaving you without a single speech!

Poor little leech,
Yes, two-legged leech,
Indeed, a proud living bitch,
Whose confidence unreached,
Wait for the life-changing twist!

THE GIRAFFE AND THE BEE

Once upon a time
there was a bee,
living on a tall tree,
making some honey.

This bee had a sweet tongue,
but mind you, he has a fang,
he's good to you when he needs you,
but betrays you with a bang!

One day a proud giraffe came,
Meeting the bee without shame,
"Hello, poor little bee,
Why do you look so ugly?"

"How dare you, giant beast!
What gave you guts to tease,
An adorable bee like me?"
Answered the boastful bee.

The two exchanged insults,
and had angry outbursts.
Suddenly, they came to realize,
that each of them should apologize.

The giraffe and the bee
became close friends,
I mean...plastic friends,
whose evil acts must end.

SNAKES AND LADDERS

Sometimes you find an epitome of
Negativity and bad vibes,
A traumatic person, you thought is
Kind and honest to you. In reality,
Every goodness he shows is a
Symbol of betrayals and bites!

Always be cautious with people-
Not all of them are safe to be with,
Dices roll and they drag you down!

Let them do the badmouthing
And the character assassination.
Don't be afraid because God is
Doing greater things for you.
Every fallen teardrop will
Refresh your heart and soul,
Soon, your miseries will lift you up!

ANTS

You are small, wingless insects
But you live in a highly organized colony
Your unmatched spirit of diligence
Is like the sun rising with its energy

You have no wise rulers
Yet you live with unity and thoroughness
Working busy in almost all hours
Actively gathering foods but not tensed

Mysterious and enigmatic you are
For you show men how to live in perfect unity
And when heavy rains shower the earth
The fruits of your labour seem so bounty

I think you are amazing engineers
The builders of your tunneled kingdom
How I wish we could be like you
No kings, no slaves but deserve freedom

Chapter 2

Salamin, Buhay at Tula
(Mirror, Life, and Poems)

PANIKI

O kaibigang paniki
bakit hindi mapakali?
Siguro'y nag-iisip kung saan sasali-
Sa mga ibon o mga hayop ba?
Dali! Bilisan mong pumili!

Ikaw naman kasi
Masyadong bilib sa sarili
Ginamit ang maiitim na pakpak mo
Upang sa mga ibon ikaw ay makasali
at magmukhang mataas at nakawiwili!

Gayundin, ang tusong paniki,
Nang ang mga ibon ay magapi,
Sa mga hayop naman kumampi,
Sinabing mga daga'y kanyang kalahi,
Upang makaiwas sa pagkamuhi!

Magpakatotoo ka na paniki,
'Di pwedeng sa dalawang panig ka sumali,
Kung wala kang paninindigan,
mas madali ka nilang magagapi,
tandaan mong nasa huli ang pagsisisi.

ALIMANGO

Pandemya man o hindi
si Alimango'y nagkukubli
ang puso'y puno ng pagkamuhi
sa kanyang kapwa'y 'di nawiwili

Nakakatakot ang sumabay
sa kanyang paglalakbay
Baka ikaw ay kanyang hilain,
duduruging pino't sisirain.

Si Alimango'y may ibang galak
kung kapwa'y lumalagapak
Kasiyahan niyang tumapak
sa mga nabalian ng pakpak.

Mag-ingat lang alimango,
Baka may nag-aabang sa iyo
Hindi mo mamamalayang
Ikaw na pala'y nanghihinayang.

MANOK

Isang kahig, isang tuka
Si manok na kawawa
Dumating pa ang pandemya
Kaya mas lalo siyang natulala

Maghapon siyang kumakayod
Halos mabiyak ang mga tuhod
Ngunit hindi basta sumusuko
Patuloy sa pagbabanat-buto

Pandemya man ay dumating
Di natinag, lumalaban pa rin
Patuloy ang laban at pangarap
Upang tagumpay ay mahanap

TUTUBI

Lumilipad mga mumunting tutubi
Sa bukid ay hindi sila mapakali
Kumulimlim ang langit at mga ulap
At bigla akong naglakbay sa alapaap

Ang mga tao'y parang mga tutubi
Na sa bayrus lahat ay nagkubli
Ayaw lumabas baka mahawa pa
At tuluyang magapi ang resistensya

Mabuti sana kung walang pamilya
Na sa kanila'y naghihintay at umaasa
Mabuti sana kung ang kalaba'y nakikita
Upang maiwasan at wag mahawa

Tayong lahat ay mga tutubi
Nagtatago man at nagkukubli
Hindi sumusuko, matatag lagi
Patuloy ang laban, di pagagapi

KABAYONG NAGBALATKAYO

Siya'y isang kabayo
Akala mo sa iyo'y totoo
'Yun pala'y nagbalat-kayo
Para ikaw ay kanyang maloko

Nagsuot ng maskara ang tusong kabayo
Upang maikubli ang kasamaan nito
Subalit nabubunyag lahat ng sikreto
Kusang umalingasaw ang baho nito

Siya pa man di'y gumamit ng pabango
Subalit ang halimuyak ay sadyang mabaho
Magaling man siyang nagbalat-kayo
Kusang lumabas ang tunay na anyo

Kaibigan, wag kang magbalat-kayo
Bakit hindi na lang magpakatotoo
Upang maging malaya't di nagtatago
At kawiwilian pa ng kapwa mo.

ASO

Si Maria ay may bagong alaga
Sa kapitbahay, mahilig gumala
Masayahin, nawiwiling makibarkada
Sa mga lansangan lumaki at tumaba

Kung kakilala ka, ito ay napakabait
Pero madalas ito ay masungit
Mahilig sa maganda, ayaw sa pangit
Kapag naiipit, kumakagat, nagagalit

Tahol nang tahol itong aso
Katulad niya ang isang kaibigan ko
Kapag nakaharap nakangiti ito
'Pag nakatalikod, bubungisngis naman ng todo

Ang aso ay maamo kapag may gusto
Sunud-sunuran kung binubusog ito
Kapag nakaharap naman ng ibang amo
Kaaway na agad ang turing sa iyo

May mga tao ring makamandag
Tulad ng asong baliw at duwag
Kung haharapin nama'y tatakbo agad
Isa ngang kaibigan, maturingang huwad

ANAY

Maliit siya
Malambot at mabagal gumalaw
Ngunit kayang gibain
Ang bahay kubo ni Mang Juan

Paunti-unting bumibiktima
Di gaano mapapansin
Isa siyang kaaway
na lihim
Na nakatago sa dilim

Ano kayang meron
Sa laway at ngipin niya
May mabisa bang sandata
Itong insektong mapanira?

Anay din daw sa lipunan
Ang mga taong mapagsamantala
Nangungulimbat at nangungurakot
Sa abang Inang Bayan

Anay din ang tawag
Sa mga taong walang silbi
Mangingilikil at magnanakaw-
Mga salot sa lipunan

PARUPARO

Saan ka nagmula
Di ba ikaw yung dating uod
Na pangit at masiba
Sa mga berdeng. dahon?
Wala kang pinipiling dahon
Hanggang sa mabusog, lumaki, lumusog
At nang naumay ka, namahinga
Binalot mo ang sarili
Natulog nang mahimbing
Ngunit isang araw, namisa ka
Lumabas sa iyong lungga
May pakpak, makulay, nakakaiba
Lumilipad, nilalang na malaya

Sana, maging katulad ka
Ang mga batang pasaway ngayon
Na habang tumatanda, nagbabago
At maging matagumpay sa buhay
At maging malaya, tulad mo

Chapter 3

Dandaniw Pagpampanunotan *(Reflection Poems in Ilocano)*

ALIBOT

Adda maysa nga abut,
Nalengdan ti ruruot,
Siniripko ket makapakigtot,
Adda idiay ni alibot!

Nabannog sa isuna
A napan nakikaarruba,
Napeklan a tsismosa,
Dilana't adda pisangna

Agbannikes ni alibot
Sa bigla nga agsuyaab,
Makaturturog piman,
Ta awan met inna naganab!

Ita kitam ket nakarungiit,
madamdama aginsasangit,
Ti ammona matuknona't langit,
Ngem dakes met ti inna naapit!

Aglemmengka lattan alibot,
Danggayam dagiti anay a naangot
Atipaem ta ngiwat ken karabukob,
Ta baka maltutanka a nailunod!

TAKONG
(Ti Bula a Nagbalin a Takong)

adu nga aramidmo ti nakaskasdaaw
kasano a natuknom
ti langit?
kasano a naballasiwmo
ti taaw?

sika't nagubbogan ken nagtaudan
ti nagpaiduma a kinalapsat
pagrukbabandaka ti amin
uray pay naangdod
ti pay-odmo, kabsat!

naisangsangayanka
ket narigat nga artapan
dagiti nagkaadu a nagpasaram!

daydi brusko ken nataer a bula,
napan inay-ayam ti panawen,
pudotna nasebsebanen!

riknana nagbaliwen,
babai metten!

agriing koman daytoy a gayyem!

TEKKA

limneken ni Apo Init
ket umarakupen ni ladingit
matitileng dagiti lapayag
kadagiti aweng a madi agbayag.

iti apagdarikmat, nagpukawen
dagiti naimbalitokan a tawen
ngem ni tekka adda pay laeng
ammona dagiti sagsagabaen.

kaariek dagiti dadduma
ngem saanak pulos nagdudua
gapu't nasin-aw a pusona
a pagubbogan ti namnama.

ti pudno a gayyem ket kasla tekka
mapagtalkan ken nakakapet kenka
uray pay naringgor no dadduma
gapu iti kanayon a pammalagipna

wen, ti pudno a gayyem ket tekka
naisangsangayan, naidumduma
numanpay kabuteng ti dadduma
sigurado a napudno kenka

BUAYA

Daytan tay crocodile tears a kunada,
Aginsasangit ngem agpagpaggaak kaungganna,
Kasla agpaypayso amin nga ibagbagana,
Pati aligusgos ket mayakarna!

No nakasango nakasaysayaat isuna,
No agsao, anghel ti kayariganna,
Ngem no nakalikodkan ket sekbabennaka,
Gundawayan ket alun-onennaka!

Appaunayen daytoy a buaya,
Arigna tay best actress iti drama,
Nagbuteng a kakuyog ken kadkadua,
Ta no dim' mapuotan ikarunokonnaka!

Masalbar ngata pay ti kararuana,
Daytoy nadakes ken nadangro a buaya?
Mapasubli ken madalusan pay ngata,
Toy aglatlati ken bubuoten a kararuana?

IGAT

Saanko makita nga agngiit,
ni pagayam nga ingget ngisit,
maamak kano ta baka mapis-it,
tay iyal-alikakana a buksit!

Dinamagko no apay agpapaigid,
ket mangrugi metten nga agsangit,
Kanayon kano a matagtagibassit,
isu a pusona kan' ti agladladingit.

Dagiti luana ket ingget pait,
ti biagna kasla makupkuppit,
maparparigatan ken maip-ipit,
ta kanayon met a mailuplupit!

Kaasi met ni pagayam nga igat,
Ta kanayon a maparparigat,
Arapaapna ngata ket maragpat,
No dagiti pannubok di mapugpugsat?

Ala, agan-anus koma latta ni igat,
Ta dumtengto kenkuana ti ragsak,
Kararagko, inna koma maragpat
Ayat ken kapia iti amin a bigat

PANIKI

O kaibigang paniki
bakit hindi mapakali?
Siguro'y nag-iisip kung saan sasali-
Sa mga ibon o mga hayop ba?
Dali! Bilisan mong pumili!

Ikaw naman kasi
Masyadong bilib sa sarili
Ginamit ang maiitim na pakpak mo
Upang sa mga ibon ikaw ay makasali
at magmukhang mataas at nakawiwili!

Gayundin, ang tusong paniki,
Nang ang mga ibon ay magapi,
Sa mga hayop naman kumampi,
Sinabing mga daga'y kanyang kalahi,
Upang makaiwas sa pagkamuhi!

Magpakatotoo ka na paniki,
'Di pwedeng sa dalawang panig ka sumali,
Kung wala kang paninindigan,
mas madali ka nilang magagapi,
tandaan mong nasa huli ang pagsisisi.

BANIAS

Nakitak a nagkarayam
daytoy gangannaet a pagayam,
Gayakgakna't di mabmabsat,
Ti ammonan nakalaplapsat!

Rumuar iti rabii,
A mapan makidingdingli,
Makikadua't saba-sabali,
Uray naasawaan a lallaki!

'Di mabayag tianna' t bimsog,
Ti ammok lang ket nabsog,
Ayna saan gayam, pordios,
Ta ni Garampang nagsikog!

Nalpasen ti panagganas,
Pagayammi a banias,
Ita kasanom a makalasat,
Iti desdes ti kinamalas?

UPPAT A RUPA TI ULEG
(4 Haiku)

(1)
Agrusrusngiit...
Agsagsagana gayam
a sumekbaben!

(2)
Aginsasangit...
Pangalana't simpatia,
mangal-allilaw!

(3)
Nakais-isem...
Gayam agkuskusilap
iti likudan!

(4)
Pumutputipot...
Pairut a pairut
a manggundaway!

SONETO PARA KENKA SUNGGO!

Kitam ta langam dita sarming,
Ingget lapsat, awan umasping.
Ngem ti naguneg anian, ading,
Nagrugit, naglidem, tinaramitim!

No sumango. sika't nakaisem,
No lumikod aglibbi, rupam ti naalsem.
No agsaoka kasla anghel kinasam-it,
Pwe! napeklanka met gayam a plastik!

Isardengmon dayta a kinaapal,
ken ta siping a dilam amangan agngadal
Isardengmo payen ti aguy-uyaw,
Baka mapukawmo bukodmo a dayaw!

O sunggo a nakabitin,
Rugiamon ti agbabawin!

TI ABBONG RUPA (FACEMASK)

Nagkarayam ti angol a mangdidigra
Nabileg a kabusor a di makitkita
Adu a wagas ti pinarnuay ti tattao
Tapno maliklikan daytoy a delubyo

Naipakdaar iti panagabbong rupa
Nangruna no mapan kadagiti kalsada
Ta malang-ab kano ti sakit a nakaro
Maysa a Pandemia a kabutbuteng ti tattao

Adda dagiti facemask a magatgatang
Adda met dagiti naanus, agdaitda lattan
Ti napateg, ti rupa maabbongan
Tapno iti Covid, ditayo maakaran

Ngarud kanayontayo koma nga agannad
Tapno masalakniban pateg ti salun-at
Iruam ti ag- facemask para iti pagimbagan
Ta daytoy ket wagas ti pannakidangadang

Kabaelantayo a paksiaten daytoy a Covid
Kas pannakaabak ni Goliath gapu ken David
Agbalin tayo a natulnog, usaren ti sirib
Tapno mapaksiattayo agraraira a sakit

KAS ITI ULEG

Ti kuna kaniak idi ni Uliteg
Iti bakir ti apon dagiti uleg
Ngem ti uleg addada met itan
Uray iti ciudad a kapintasan

Ngem ti uleg dida mangan-ano
Kasta ti kuna ni Lelongko
Agtiliwdakan iti bao
Nga agperdi iti mulatayo

Ngem nakaam-amak ti gitada
Ipatay no di sigud masuma
Gapuna agan-annadtayo koma
Kadagiti uleg nga agkaiwara

Uleg ti awagda iti mangliliput
A mangsabidong puso ken panunot
Gapuna agsiputka ngarud
Kadagiti uleg a mangiluod

No dadduma dagiti uleg agkikinnagat
Iladawanda't galad a nalaad
Gapuna makikaduaka a siaannad
Ta amangan no ti gayyem karasaen a naranggas
ipakitam man dayta

TI TUKAK

Natibong manen uni dagiti tukak
Agsasarakda iti pilaw wenno lubnak
Kasta ngamin no adda bayakabak
Agpipinnukkawda iti rabaw ti tambak

Ti tukak naragsakda no adda tudo
Agfiestada iti apagkanito
Ngem no bumaybayag, maumadanto
Dayta ti wagasda, maysa a kinapudno

Naanus ketdi dagiti tukak
Nga agibtur iti nakaro a tikag
Aglemmengda iti nasamek a bangkag
A manguray gundawayda nga agragsak

Ay, tukaknak man la koma
A mapnek iti bassit nga adda
Ta umanayen a makaliwliwa
Dagiti agtennag, maiyarbis a grasiA

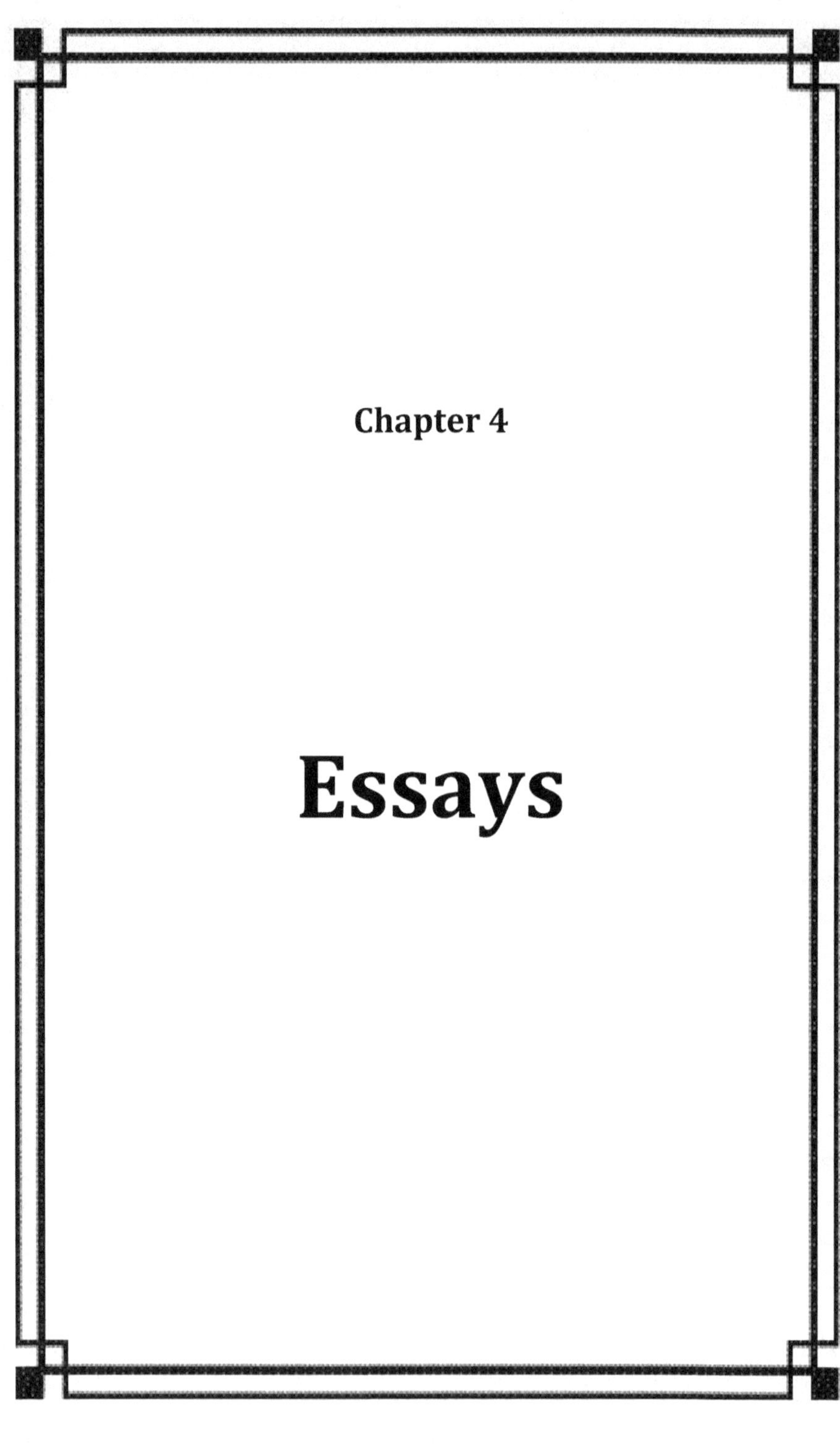

Chapter 4

Essays

PUNCTUATIONS OF LIFE

Life is full of challenges. These challenges make life more interesting and meaningful. As what motivational writer Roy Bennett said, every challenge, every adversity, contains within it the seeds of opportunity and growth. Thus, looking at the brighter side, overcoming challenges gives us wisdom and molds us to be better individuals.

However, some people do not think this way. Sometimes, their challenges led them to anxiety, depression, and even suicide. With this in mind, I wrote this simple article to promote holistic mental health for all. In this simple way, I might help our fellow who is suffering from depression.

Do you know that five punctuation marks would leave us a message of positivism and hope?

Let's start with a question mark (?). There might be a lot of questions in your mind. These questions give us emotional disturbances because sometimes, the answers to these questions seem to be unacceptable. Sometimes, we even question God why tragic things happen. Yes, we loosen our firm faith and start to break into pieces.

Aside from a question mark, an exclamation mark (!) gives us great symbolism in life. An exclamation mark reminds us to be cautious in all our actions. It is like an alarm that would awaken our souls at times of danger. Yes, life is basically dangerous but if you rekindle your faith in Him, you will never be destroyed.

Question and exclamation marks may disturb your mind and may lead you to a period (.). But no, life must go on. In my article, the period wasn't placed in the end because ending your life should never be the last option. Keep in mind that if there is one reason to give up, there are more reasons to keep going.

Never lose hope. A comma (,) is always there to remind you to take a break and to pause for a while. Find time to reflect and to reminisce the beautiful memories; to think of the people who genuinely love and admire you, and to appreciate that life is a beautiful gift from God.

So, never end life with a period. Instead, end it with an ellipsis (...) which symbolizes continuity, opportunities, and growth. Be strong and resilient at all times. Never let a failure or a disappointment end your dreams. At the end of the day, life is a blessing to treasure and enjoy.

A SPECTRUM OF REALITY

What comes into your mind when you hear the acronym ROYGBIV? I'm sure that a rainbow automatically pops out in your mind. Yes, ROYGBIV is an acronym for a sequence of hues commonly described as making up a rainbow: red, orange, yellow, green, blue, indigo and violet. But have you ever thought that these hues actually represent 7 realities in life?

Life is...

Red. This hue represents love and courage in life. I remember a beautiful line from Alfred Lord Tennyson - "'Tis better to have loved and lost than never to have loved at all". Indeed, when your love story didn't end the way you wanted it to be, turn your red hue of love into courage. Have that courage to overcome the challenges and be the best version of yourself. Someday somehow, the right person will come to you unexpectedly.

Orange. This hue reminds us of life's energy, vitality, and adventure. What is life without these three?! I remember a quotation from Alfred North Whitehead - "The vitality of thought is in adventure. Ideas won't keep. Something must be done about them. When the idea is new, its custodians have fervor, live for it, and if need be, die for it." So, never settle for less and always keep the positive energy to conquer all your dreams.

Yellow. This hue brings happiness and optimism. In life, these two are very essential in order to successfully hurdle challenges and adversities. According to Roy Bennett, it's only after you've stepped outside your comfort zone that you begin to change, grow, and transform. So, wear your coats of happiness and optimism and be the best you can be!

Green. This hue reflects generosity, kindness, and compassion. These values are essential during these times of crisis. As Amelia

Earheart once said, "A single act of kindness throws out roots in all directions, and the roots spring up and make new trees." So, be a sturdy tree that will spread generosity and you will be remembered forever.

Blue. This hue illuminates serenity and stability. Sometimes, even the deep blue sea turns chaotic and stormy. Life, too, is not always a bed of roses because there are thorns in it. However, I remember a famous line from the great Dalai Lama - "Inner peace is the key: if you have inner peace, the external problems do not affect your deep sense of peace and tranquility. Without this inner peace, no matter how comfortable your life is materially, you may still be worried, disturbed, or unhappy because of circumstances." So, if you wish for a calm and peaceful life, have that inner peace in you.

Indigo. This hue conveys integrity and deep sincerity. I learned in life that people will forget what you said, people will forget what you did, but people will never forget how you made them feel. I remember a quotation from Oprah Winfrey- "Real integrity is doing the right thing, knowing that nobody's going to know whether you did it or not." Indeed, you have to protect your integrity at all times.

Violet. This hue reveals innocence and humility. In life, innocence and humility will keep you safe and respected. As Ralph Waldo Emerson once said, "A great man is always willing to be little." Indeed, a humble and meek person will always be uplifted by the people he had inspired. So, be a person of humility at all times.

Always remember your ROYGBIV and start creating a rainbow of your new and better self.

PANDEMIC DIRGE

"I wept because I had no shoes until I saw a man who had no feet."

This beautiful line from Robin Sharma's 'WHO WILL CRY WHEN YOU DIE?' teaches us essential values that we need to possess during these trying times of the pandemic.

Life has been so challenging not only because of the potential threats of the virus but because most of us were now infected with the deadly 3Bs: Bitching, Badmouthing, and Backstabbing.

The book teaches us five essential values to overcome these 3Bs. First, it teaches us to BE HONEST. One of the reasons why the virus had spread easily is that we were untruthful. We became bitches of different colors and liars of different breeds. It is high time to realize that every single lie that we tell is a serious threat to humanity.

Second, it teaches us to BE MORE LOVING. Love should be an investment for everyone. Every small gesture of kindness that we do is a thing of joy that would make others feel that they are loved. As Robin Sharma quoted: "Kindness, quite simply, is the rent we must pay for the space we occupy on the planet."

Third, it teaches us to BE HUMBLE. Being meek will never bring us down. Having that humble personality is something that people will always treasure about us.

Fourth, it teaches us to BE FORGIVING. Never invest hatred in others. Always wear that positive vibe. Let us always keep the positive spirit in our hearts. Let us keep it burning so that we ignite our passion to achieve our goals and aspirations.

Lastly, it teaches us to BE THANKFUL. We should stop worrying about the things that we wish never happened to us like this pandemic. Instead, we just look into the brighter side of it... we failed to see that the pandemic had also strengthened our familial bonds and ties and that it made us more resilient than before.

Ask yourself now. Who will really cry when you die? If you don't know the answer yet, BE HONEST, BE MORE LOVING, BE HUMBLE, BE FORGIVING, and BE THANKFUL.

About the Author:

Mark Angelo Rivera Damo is a Senior High School
English Language and Literature teacher
of San Nicolas National High School,
San Nicolas, Ilocos Norte. He graduated
Cum Laude of the degree Bachelor in Secondary
Education major in English at the Mariano Marcos
State University- College of Teacher Education.
He is an award-winning writer, school paper
adviser and journalism coach.